D1549917

C015561015

Published in paperback in 2013 by Wayland
Text copyright © Pat Thomas 2013
Illustrations copyright © Lesley Harker 2013

Wayland
Hachette Children's Books
338, Euston Road,
London NW1 3BH

Wayland Australia
Level 17/207 Kent Street
Sydney, NSW 2000

Concept design: Kate Buxton
Series design: Elaine Wilkinson

British Library Cataloguing in Publication Data
Thomas, Pat, 1959-
I can do it! : a first look at not giving up. -- (A first
look at)
1. Determination (Personality trait)--Juvenile literature.
2. Achievement motivation--Juvenile literature.
I. Title II. Series
153.8-dc22

ISBN: 978 0 7502 7140 0

Printed in China

Wayland is a division of Hachette Children's Books,
an Hachette UK company.
www.hachette.co.uk

I can do it!

A FIRST LOOK AT NOT GIVING UP

PAT THOMAS
ILLUSTRATED BY LESLEY HARKER

WAYLAND

Have you ever tried
to do something that
was really hard?

So hard that you felt like you wanted to give up?

7

Everybody enjoys doing things that are easy,
and that they are good at.

Sometimes it's hard to understand why you should keep trying to do something that seems quite hard at first.

Learning to do new things makes
life more interesting.

It also makes us more interesting people to be
around and more able to help and take part
in the things going on around us.

But learning anything new often takes patience
and practice – even for grown-ups.

What about you?

Can you think of some things you've tried that have been hard?

Did you give up or did you keep trying?

Whether you are learning a new sport or how to play an instrument, or doing a maths problem or a puzzle, or trying to figure out how to play a new game.

If you want to get better
at it, you need to keep
at it and keep finding
different ways to
get better.

Most of us don't get things right –
or do them well – the first time we try.

When you don't get something right the
first time it's normal to feel frustrated
and sad and cross.

But don't let that stop you from
trying again.

Thinking that you can't do it can make getting it right even harder.

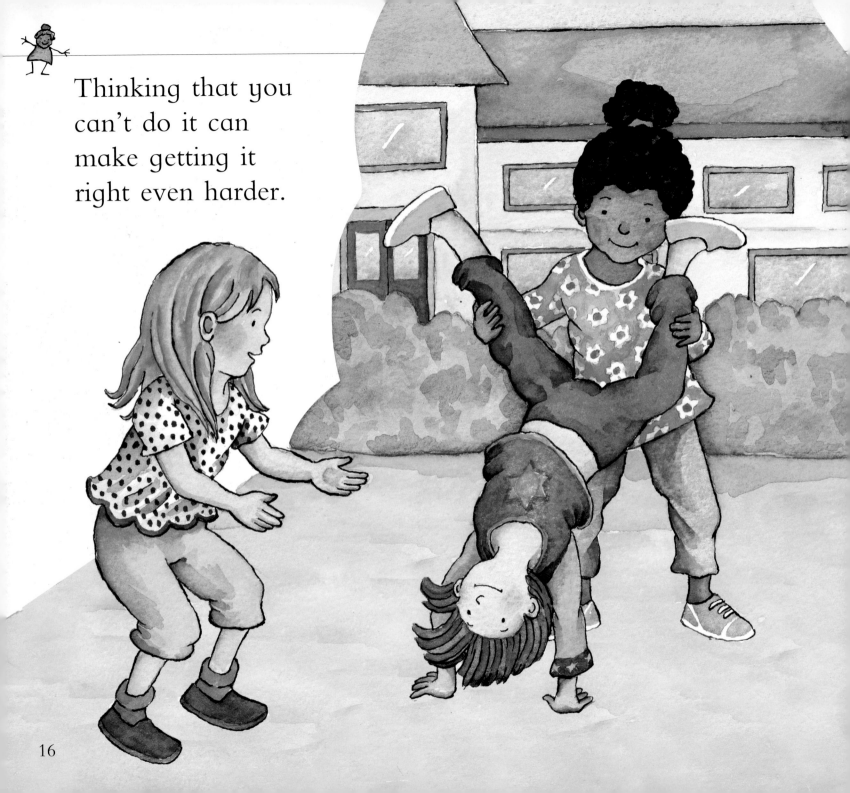

So always try to tell yourself 'I can do it'.

And listen to others when they encourage you and tell you that they believe in you, too.

17

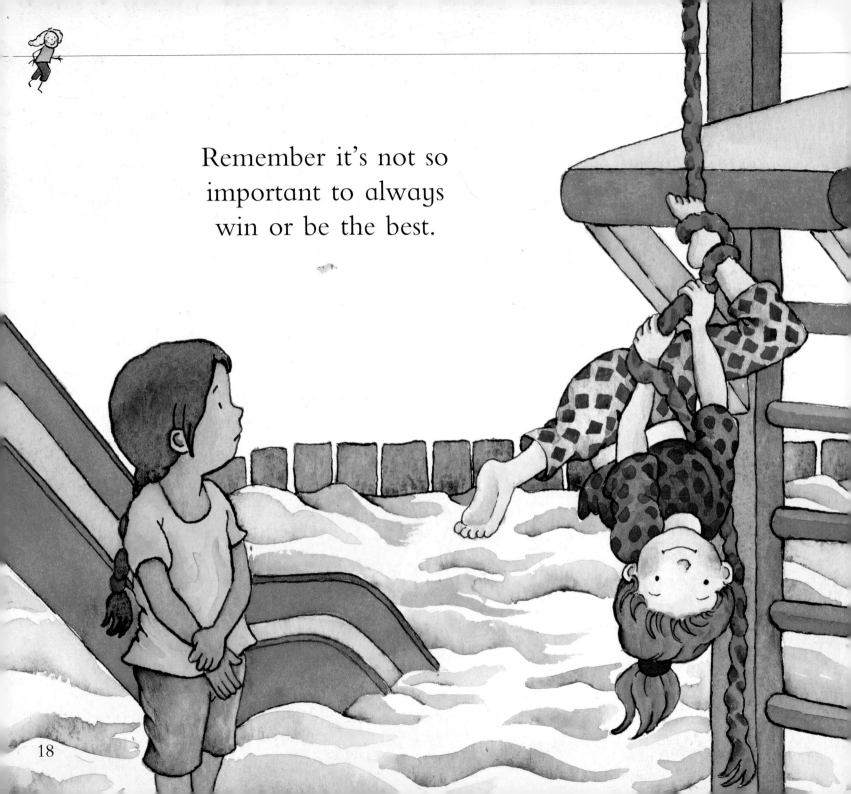

Remember it's not so
important to always
win or be the best.

It's more important to always do your best and to finish what you have started.

No matter what you are doing,
when you know you have tried your best
then you can be really proud of yourself.

And your friends and family
will be proud of you too.

What about you?

Do you think it is always important to win? How does it feel when
you can't do something well? Can you think of some times when
you didn't win, but you felt proud that you tried really hard?

Some people only ever do the things
they know they will be good at.

They never try anything
new because they are afraid they might fail.

Or they are afraid that
people might make
fun of them.

Or they might let their friends and families down.

But trying new things is part of life.

It teaches you new skills, helps you to find new ways of solving problems and gives you confidence.

Life would be pretty boring if we
only ever did the things that were easy,
or played the games we knew we could.

So try not to be afraid
of things that seem
hard at first.

With a little effort you may just find they are the things you enjoy doing the most.

HOW TO USE THIS BOOK

This book provides a basic introduction to the concept of perseverance. You can reinforce its message by providing day-to-day lessons in perseverance for your child. When you teach your child to persevere you are giving them an important practical and emotional skill that will help them throughout their lives. While some children find it easier to stick at things than others, all can learn some aspects of this trait.

As with any new skill, it's important to make the lesson fun and age appropriate. Young children can be encouraged to finish or complete a craft project or persevere with a puzzle. Small achievable goals can produce a big sense of achievement. As they get older let your child lead by deciding what he or she wants to achieve next - whether it's learning to skate or swim or just getting to the top of the climbing frame - and let them go at their own pace. Instead of jumping in immediately when they are struggling, try to cheer from the sidelines. Letting your child know that you have faith in their ability to figure things out can boost self-esteem and provide the encouragement needed to finish things.

Children learn by example, so make sure you include your child in your own goal-setting behaviour. Adults understand how to break down complex tasks and goals into smaller steps, and showing how this process works passes an important skill on to your child.
Be aware of family language as well, as how it can reinforce defeatism. Phrases like "I can't..." and "I'll never..." can make everyone feel like giving up. Saying "I know I can do it!" and "I don't want to give up",

and even truisms like "Winners never quit, quitters never win," and, "If at first you don't succeed, try, try again!" help keep a positive frame of mind.

At the same time keep an eye on the bigger picture of why you might want your child to persevere. Is it because you want your child to be the 'best' in comparison to others, to win medals and external praise, or to do his or her 'best' and feel a sense of personal achievement? Be aware also of asking children to persevere with things that clearly make them unhappy. When your child does persevere, show them that you're proud of their commitment, effort and determination above and beyond any trophy, grade or medal they might get.

In the classroom teachers can lead discussions on what perseverance means and does not mean. For example: keep working until the assignment is complete, instead of trying only a few times and quitting. With the help of students list the steps that are needed to learn a new skill such as riding a bicycle, learning to swim or memorising times tables. Students can also write or draw a picture illustrating a time when they persevered and succeeded even though they felt like giving up and then discuss the feelings associated with their achievement. Stories about perseverance can provide good topics for reports and discussions; as are biographies of real life people such Albert Einstein, Helen Keller, Thomas Edison, Mother Teresa and Madame (Marie) Curie. School visits and talks from a respected community member who overcame obstacles can make the lesson more 'real'.

BOOKS TO READ

Never Give Up: Learning about Perseverance
Regina Burch (Creative Teaching Press, 2002)

Dog Tired: A Learning Adventure in Perseverance
Tony Salerno (New Leaf Press, 2005)

Horton Hatches the Egg, Dr. Seuss
(HarperCollins Children's Books, 2004)

I'll do It: Taking Responsibility
Mike Gordon (Wayland, 1998)

The Little Engine that Could
Watty Piper (G P Putnam's Sons, 2002)

The Very Busy Spider
Eric Carle (Grosset & Dunlap, 2006)

Stuart Little
E.B. White (Puffin, 2007)

The Children's Book of Virtues
William J Bennett (Simon & Schuster 1996)

RESOURCES FOR ADULTS

**The Values Book: Teaching Sixteen Basic Values
   to Young Children**
Pam Schiller, Tamera Bryant (Gryphon House, 1998)

Teaching Your Children Values
Lind and Richard Eyre (Fireside, 1993)

**The Book of Virtues: a Treasury of great moral
   stories**
William J Bennett (Simon & Schuster 1993)

What Do You Stand For?
Barbara A Lewis (Free Spirit, 1998)